Pupil Book 4B

D1638100

Series Editor: Peter Clarke

Authors: Elizabeth Jurgensen, Jeanette Mumford, Sandra Roberts

Contents

Ordering numbers beyond 1000

Order and compare numbers beyond 1000

Challenge 1

1 Order each set of numbers, smallest to largest.

   a 3871, 2356, 1736, 5197   **b** 5812, 3982, 2645, 1836

   c 4876, 1088, 3721, 2677   **d** 5222, 3121, 1889, 2776

2 Order each set of numbers, smallest to largest.
Look at the 100s digits to help you.

> **Example**
> 3185, 3288, 3346, 3409

   a 1487, 1289, 1578, 1065   **b** 3825, 3166, 3498, 3255

   c 5538, 5216, 5754, 5111   **d** 4622, 4826, 4286, 4166

Challenge 2

1 Order each set of numbers, smallest to largest.

   a 4879, 2789, 4791, 2178   **b** 6372, 6187, 4277, 4722

   c 3981, 3521, 3734, 3143   **d** 8256, 7256, 8454, 7454

2 For each number on these whiteboards, write one 4-digit number that is smaller and one that is larger.

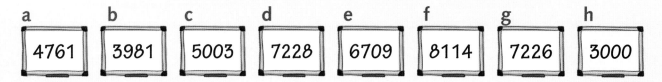

a	b	c	d	e	f	g	h
4761	3981	5003	7228	6709	8114	7226	3000

Challenge 3

1 Write a set of instructions for ordering 4-digit numbers.

2 Using the cards, make two 4-digit numbers that are smaller and two 4-digit numbers that are larger than each of the numbers on the whiteboards above.

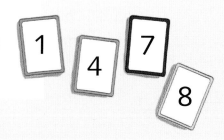

Place value problems

Solve number and practical problems that involve place value

Challenge 1

Using the 1–3 spinner, reduce each 3-digit number to 0 in ten spins or fewer. Write the numbers you subtract and record your new number each time. You can subtract 100s, 10s or 1s.

a 647   **b** 586   **c** 739   **d** 578   **e** 483

You will need:
• Resource 7: 1–3 spinner

I spun 2 so I can subtract 200 or 20 or 2.

Challenge 2

1 Using the 1–3 spinner, reduce each 4-digit number to 0 in ten spins or fewer. Write the numbers you subtract and record your new number each time. You can subtract 1000s, 100s, 10s or 1s.

a 3562   **b** 4271   **c** 4854   **d** 5311   **e** 5924

2 Explain how you chose which digit to reduce each time.

I hope I spin 1 so I can change the 1000s digit to 0.

Example

$$
\begin{array}{r}
4257 \\
-\ 200 \\
\hline
4057 \\
-\ 3000 \\
\hline
1057 \\
-\ 2 \\
\hline
1055
\end{array}
$$

Challenge 3

1 Using a 1–6 dice, reduce each number to 0 in ten rolls or fewer. Write the numbers you subtract and record your new number each time. You can subtract 1000s, 100s, 10s or 1s.

You will need:
• 1–6 dice

a 5734   **b** 6483   **c** 8657   **d** 9248   **e** 7835

2 Play this game with a partner.

• You and your partner choose the same 4-digit start number and write it down.
• Take turns to roll the dice.
• Choose the 1000s, 100s, 10s or 1s digit and reduce your number.
• The first to reduce their number to 0 is the winner.

Rounding to the nearest 10 or 100

Round any number to the nearest 10 or 100

Challenge 1

1 Write the two multiples of 10 that each number comes between on either side of the number.

a	147	b	189	c	231	d	358

e	725	f	866	g	673	h	744

2 Now look at the 1s digit and decide whether the number should be rounded up or down. Circle the correct multiple of 10.

Example

460←468→470

460←468→(470)

Challenge 2

1 Write the two multiples of 10 that each number comes between on either side of the number.

a 875 b 749 c 1837 d 2568 e 2371

2 Now look at the 1s digit and decide whether the number should be rounded up or down. Circle the correct multiple of 10.

3 Write the two multiples of 100 that each number comes between on either side of the number.

a 765 b 353 c 287 d 915 e 1528

Example

400←468→500

400←468→(500)

4 Look at the 10s digit and decide whether the number should be rounded up or down. Circle the correct multiple of 100.

Challenge 3

1 Write the multiples of 10 and 100 that these numbers come between on either side of the number. Then circle the multiple of 10 and 100 that the number rounds to.

Example

(5470)↖   ↗5480
         5473
5400↙   ↘(5500)

a 2716 b 3569 c 3248 d 4635 e 7482 f 7255

2 Explain the rules for rounding numbers.

Negative numbers

Count backwards through 0 to include negative numbers

Write the missing numbers.

a −5, ___, −3, ___, ___, 0, 1, ___, 3,

b −8, ___, ___, −5, ___, −3, ___, ___, 0,

c −10, ___, ___, ___, −6, ___, ___, −3, ___, −1

d −15, ___, −13, ___, ___, ___, −9, ___, ___, −6

e −19, ___, ___, ___, −15, ___, ___, −12, ___,

f −25, ___, −23, ___, ___, ___, −19, ___, −17

g −28, ___, ___, ___, −24, ___, ___, ___, −20,

1 Counting backwards, write the next number after:

a −7   b −1   c −4   d −10   e −13   f −17   g −21   h −29

2 Start at these numbers and count back 5 numbers.
   Record your numbers on a number line.

a −20   b −18   c −21   d −24   e −33   f −39   g −46   h −50

1 Counting backwards, write the next number after:

a −38   b −42   c −47   d −50   e −56   f −59   g −64   h −71

2 Start at these numbers and count back 5 numbers.
   Record your numbers on a number line.

a −69   b −75   c −79   d −86   e −93   f −99   g −105

Subtraction chains

Use mental methods for subtraction

Copy the number chain, writing the start number at the beginning. Try to work out all the calculations mentally. Repeat for all five start numbers.

 Challenge 1   Start numbers:

    a 320   **b** 350   **c** 480   **d** 410   **e** 440

Start number → ? → ? → ? → ? → ? → ? → ?

    −30   −7   −100   −50   −3   −62   −48

 Challenge 2   Start numbers:

    a 740   **b** 770   **c** 810   **d** 850   **e** 920

Start number → ? → ? → ? → ? → ? → ? → ?

    −253   −70   −130   −7   −186   −80   −9

Challenge 3   Start numbers:

    a 1050   **b** 1140   **c** 1200   **d** 1250   **e** 1300

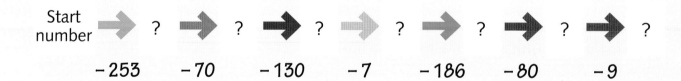

Start number → ? → ? → ? → ? → ? → ? → ?

    −372   −50   −8   −249   −167   −90   −106

Written subtraction (1)

- Subtract numbers with up to 4 digits using the formal written method of columnar subtraction
- Estimate and use inverse operations to check answers to a calculation

Challenge 1

a 574 – 251	b 675 – 432	c 682 – 356	d 574 – 248
e 636 – 318	f 754 – 329	g 766 – 548	h 827 – 419

Challenge 2

1 Write an estimate for these calculations before you work them out.

a 763 – 381	b 873 – 458	c 839 – 273	d 775 – 448
e 853 – 476	f 865 – 479	g 872 – 695	h 841 – 764

2 Choose four of your calculations and check your answers using the inverse operation.

Challenge 3

1 Write an estimate for these calculations before you work them out.

a 953 – 488	b 926 – 549	c 910 – 642	d 1267 – 1159
e 1358 – 1126	f 1326 – 1153	g 1462 – 1274	h 1514 – 1236

2 Choose four of your calculations and check your answers using the inverse operation.

9

Written subtraction (2)

- Subtract numbers with up to 4 digits using the formal written method of columnar subtraction
- Estimate and use inverse operations to check answers to a calculation

Challenge 1

a	548 – 267	b	635 – 218	c	672 – 359	d	741 – 328
e	692 – 355	f	717 – 432	g	783 – 257	h	725 – 468

Challenge 2

1 Write an estimate for these calculations before you work them out.

a	1273 – 1165	b	1149 – 1064	c	2176 – 1352	d	2268 – 1441
e	2281 – 1536	f	2435 – 1672	g	3283 – 2616	h	2753 – 2578

2 Choose four of your calculations and check your answers using the inverse operation.

3 Using the cards, make eight subtraction calculations and work them out.

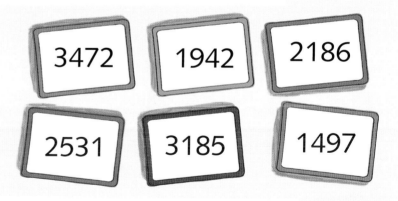

3472   1942   2186

2531   3185   1497

Challenge 3

1 Write an estimate for these calculations before you work them out.

a	3271 – 2448	b	3356 – 2781	c	3417 – 2632	d	3792 – 1876
e	4053 – 2318	f	4147 – 1519	g	4326 – 2715	h	4516 – 2738

2 Choose four of your calculations and check your answers using the inverse operation.

Trip problems

Solve 2-step problems in contexts,
deciding which operations to use and why

Challenge 1

1 On the day of the school trip, 150 Year 7 children turn up
   late and 240 turn up on time. How many Year 7s are there altogether?

2 A teacher asks how many Year 7 children have remembered to bring
   a drink. Out of 290 children, 130 put up their hand. How many
   children have forgotten their drink?

3 A teacher has a museum ticket for 378 children. 264 children have
   entered so far. How many more children can enter on the ticket?

Challenge 2

1 A teacher is counting children as they arrive at school. 254 Year 7s, 162 Year 8s
   and 307 Year 9s have arrived so far. How many children are in school?

2 The museum is expecting 746 children to go to a lecture. 258 arrive early and
   367 arrive on time. How many children are late?

3 364 children bring juice to drink, 275 bring water to drink and 378 bring squash.
   How many brought drinks?

Challenge 3

1 Travelling by train there are 47 teachers, 235 Year 7s and 365 Year 8s.
   How many people in total travel by train?

2 By 9 o'clock, 487 Year 7 children have arrived, 535 Year 8s and some Year 9s.
   1347 children are there in total. How many Year 9 children have arrived?

3 On the way back from the museum, 682 children say they have lost their
   coats and 529 children say they have lost their bags. The next day 425 items
   have been found. How many children still have missing coats and bags?

4 1263 children are asked if the trip was useful for their learning. 876 say it
   was really useful, 255 say it was mostly useful and the rest were not sure.
   How many were not sure about the trip?

Acute and obtuse angles

Identify acute and obtuse angles

You will need:
• right-angle tester

Challenges 1,2

1 Use your right-angle tester to find the acute and obtuse angles.

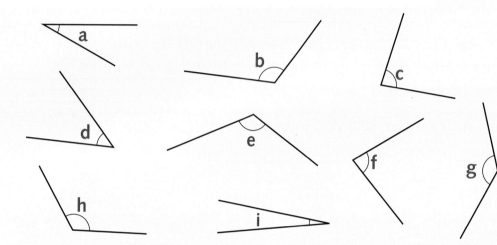

2 Copy and complete the table.

Acute angle	Obtuse angle
a,	

Challenge 3

1 List the acute and obtuse angles in the circle.

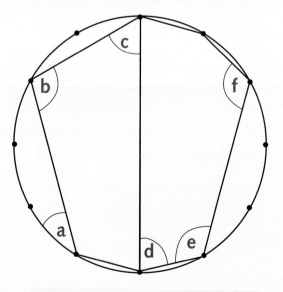

2 a Using Resource 32: 12-dot circles, investigate drawing a continuous line in a 12-dot circle which makes at least two acute and two obtuse angles.

b Colour the acute angles red and the obtuse angles blue.

You will need:
• Resource 32: 12-dot circles
• red and blue pencils

Acute and obtuse angles in 2-D shapes

Identify acute and obtuse angles in 2-D shapes

Challenge 1

Name the marked angle in each shape as acute or obtuse.

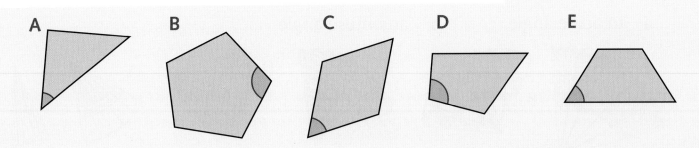

Challenge 2

Name the marked angle in each shape as acute or obtuse.

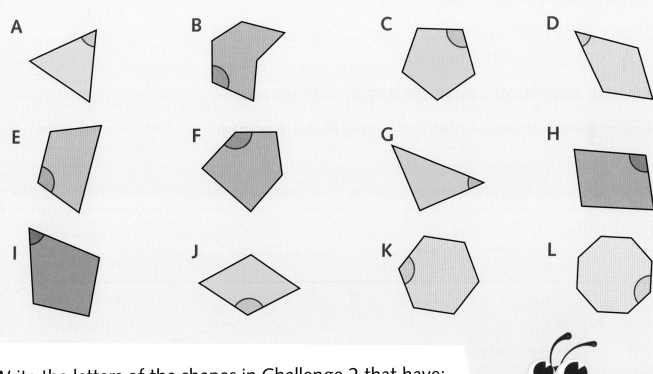

Challenge 3

Write the letters of the shapes in Challenge 2 that have:

    a at least two acute angles   **b** at least two obtuse angles

    c two pairs of acute angles and two pairs of obtuse angles

Ordering angles by size

Compare and order angles up to two right angles by size

 Challenge 1

Use your right-angle tester. Write which fans show:

You will need:
• right-angle tester

a an acute angle   **b** an obtuse angle

 Challenge 2

1 Using the right-angle tester, write all the angles that are acute in the angles below.

2 Using the right-angle tester, write all the angles that are obtuse in the angles below.

3 Using both testers, order the angles that are acute.

4 Using both testers, order the angles that are obtuse.

You will need:
• right-angle tester
• half right-angle tester

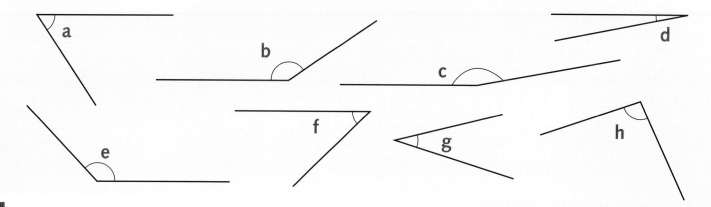

Challenge 3

Write the letter of the angle in Challenge 2 which is:

a about half a right angle   **b** about half a right angle plus a right angle

c the smallest obtuse angle   **d** the greatest acute angle

Regular polygons

Decide if a polygon is regular or irregular by comparing lengths and angles

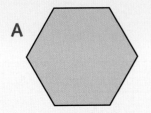

A

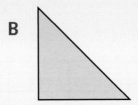

B

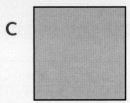

C

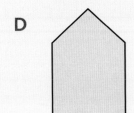

D

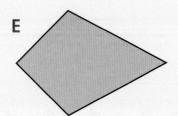

E

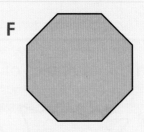

F

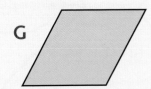

G

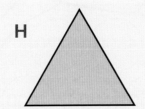

H

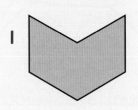

I

 Challenges 1,2

1 Use your ruler to measure the sides of each 2-D shape.
   Write the letters of the shapes which have:

You will need:
• ruler

   a all sides equal   b all angles equal

2 Copy and complete the table for shapes A to I.

	Regular	Irregular
	A,	

 Challenge 3

Look for lines of symmetry in shapes A to I and complete the table.

Property	Regular	Irregular
One line of symmetry	A,	
More than one line of symmetry		

Multiples of 25, 100 and 1000

Count in multiples of 25, 100 and 1000

Challenge 1 Write the missing numbers.

a	1000	2000							10 000
b	6100			6400				6900	
c	25		75		125				

Challenge 2 Find the multiples of 1000, 100 and 25.

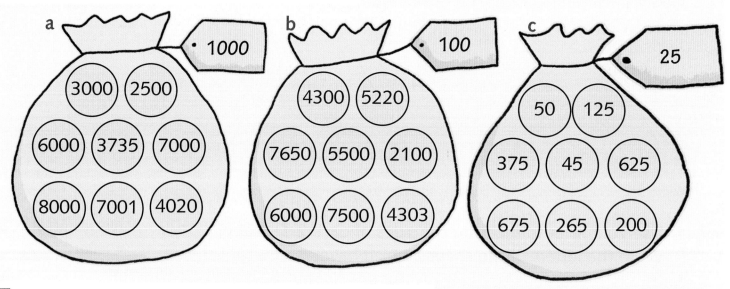

Challenge 3

1 Write a multiple of 25 that matches each clue.

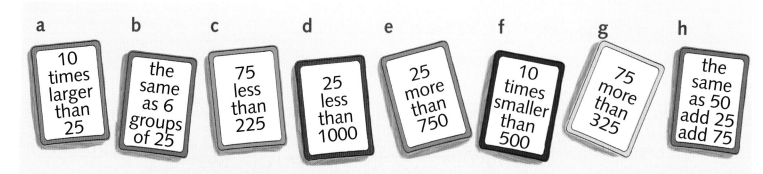

a 10 times larger than 25
b the same as 6 groups of 25
c 75 less than 225
d 25 less than 1000
e 25 more than 750
f 10 times smaller than 500
g 75 more than 325
h the same as 50 add 25 add 75

2 Make up your own multiple of 25 clue to share with a partner.

16

Multiplication using the formal written method

Use the formal written method to calculate TO × O

Challenge 1

Find the missing number in each calculation.

a $3 \times 9 = \bigcirc$ b $\square \times 6 = 36$ c $8 \times 8 = \triangle$ d $9 \times \bigcirc = 63$

e $4 \times \blacksquare = 28$ f $7 \times \triangle = 35$ g $6 \times \bullet = 48$ h $\square \times 8 = 88$

Challenge 2

Choose a number from box A and a number from box B. Multiply them together and write the answer. Make eight calculations. Choose different numbers each time.

A
36 48 49
24 32 56 28
64 72 18 54

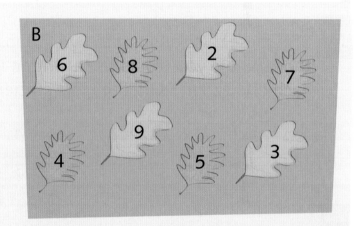

B
6 8 2 7
4 9 5 3

Challenge 3

1 Estimate the answer to each calculation.

a	b	c	d	e	f	g	h
75 × 4	63 × 8	46 × 7	84 × 4	87 × 9	59 × 5	49 × 6	76 × 8

2 Work out the answer to each of the calculations above using the formal written method of multiplication. Check your answer is close to your estimated answer.

Example

$68 \times 6 \rightarrow 70 \times 6 = 420$

H	T	O
	6	8
×		6
	4	
4	0	8

17

Multiplication using the most efficient method

Use the most efficient method to calculate TO × O

Challenge 1

Write the answers to these multiplication facts.

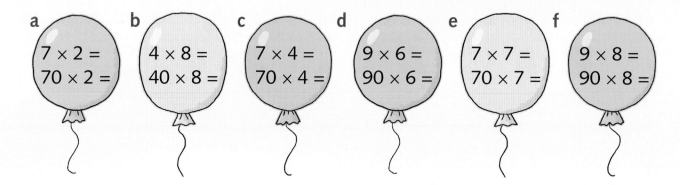

a
7 × 2 =
70 × 2 =

b
4 × 8 =
40 × 8 =

c
7 × 4 =
70 × 4 =

d
9 × 6 =
90 × 6 =

e
7 × 7 =
70 × 7 =

f
9 × 8 =
90 × 8 =

Challenge 2

Sort these calculations into two groups: those you would work out mentally and those where you would use a written method. Then work out the answer to each calculation using the most efficient method.

33 × 3	42 × 3	55 × 4	62 × 3	76 × 8	89 × 7
67 × 8	34 × 2	53 × 3	75 × 2	79 × 9	86 × 7

Challenge 3

Play this game with a partner. Each player chooses a number from the number cards. Take turns to:

- roll the 1–9 dice
- multiply the number on the dice by your chosen number
- choose the most appropriate method to calculate the answer, mental or written.

If you choose a written method, write the estimated answer first and then show your working out. Compare your answers each time. The player with the largest answer scores one point. The first player to score 5 points is the winner.

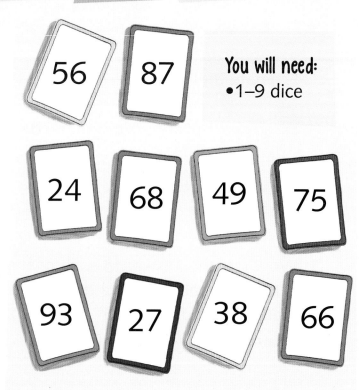

You will need:
- 1–9 dice

56   87

24   68   49   75

93   27   38   66

Solving word problems

Solve problems and reason mathematically

Answer each calculation then write the inverse multiplication or division fact.

a $24 \div 3 =$ b $6 \times 7 =$ c $8 \; 6 =$ d $54 \div 9 =$

e $7 \times 9 =$ f $7 \times 4 =$ g $32 \div 4 =$ h $56 \div 7 =$

Using the information in the pictures, write a calculation to find the total number of items in each order.

 89  74  86 63 37  95

Order a 3 boxes of calculators	**Order b** 2 boxes of rulers and 1 box of paintbrushes
Order c 2 boxes of coloured pencils	**Order d** 1 box of rulers and 1 box of calculators
Order e 2 boxes of paintbrushes	**Order f** 1 box of coloured pencils and 1 box of crayons

Use the information in the pictures above to answer the questions below.

a Glue sticks are sold in packs of 3. How many packs of glue sticks in one box?

b The school buys 8 boxes of paintbrushes. Each box costs £10. What is the total cost?

c What is the difference in the number of coloured pencils and the number of crayons in a box?

d The school needs 50 calculators but only has 1 box. How many more calculators do they need?

e Boxes of crayons come in 5 colours. How many of each colour?

f The Year 4 children need 100 glue sticks but only have 1 box. How many extra sticks do they need?

Fractions and number lines

Use the number line to connect fractions and numbers

 Challenge 1   Write the fractions that are missing from the number lines.

a 0 ————————— 1

b 0 ————————— 1

c 0 ————————— 1

d 0 ————————— 1

 Challenge 2   Write the fractions that are missing from the number lines.

a 5 ——— 6 ——— 7

b 3 ——— 4 ——— 5

c 6 ——— 7 ——— 8

d 8 ——— 9 ——— 10

e 11 ——— 12 ——— 13

f 15 ——— 16 ——— 17

 Challenge 3

1 Write the fractions that are missing from the number lines.
Use two different denominators in your fractions.

a 0 ————————— 1

b 0 ————————— 1

c 0 ————————— 1

2 Draw a number line 12 cm long. Mark the half and the quarter intervals on your number line.

Hundredths and tenths

- Count up and down in hundredths
- Recognise that hundredths arise when dividing by 100 and dividing tenths by 10

Challenge 1

Write the missing hundredths.

a $\frac{13}{100}$, $\frac{14}{100}$, ___, $\frac{16}{100}$, ___, ___, $\frac{19}{100}$, ___, $\frac{21}{100}$,

b $\frac{27}{100}$, ___, $\frac{29}{100}$, ___, ___, $\frac{32}{100}$, ___, ___, $\frac{35}{100}$,

c $\frac{62}{100}$, ___, ___, ___, $\frac{66}{100}$, ___, ___, $\frac{70}{100}$, ___

d   ___, $\frac{50}{100}$, ___, ___, ___, $\frac{54}{100}$, ___, ___, $\frac{58}{100}$

Challenge 2

1   Count on in hundredths 10 times from these fractions.

a $\frac{25}{100}$ b $\frac{38}{100}$ c $\frac{50}{100}$ d $\frac{67}{100}$ e $\frac{80}{100}$ f $\frac{86}{100}$ g $\frac{90}{100}$

2   Count back in hundredths 10 times from these fractions.

a $\frac{60}{100}$ b $\frac{81}{100}$ c $\frac{32}{100}$ d $\frac{99}{100}$ e $\frac{55}{100}$ f $\frac{73}{100}$ g $\frac{62}{100}$

3   For each 100 grid, write the fraction that is shaded blue.

 a   b   c   d   e

Challenge 3

Write a tenth and a hundredth describing what fraction of each 100 grid is shaded blue.

 a   b   c   d   e

Finding tenths and hundredths

Use multiplication and division to find non-unit tenths and hundredths

Challenge 1

1 Work out these tenths.

a $\frac{1}{10}$ of 30 b $\frac{1}{10}$ of 50 c $\frac{1}{10}$ of 60 d $\frac{1}{10}$ of 90

e $\frac{1}{10}$ of 70 f $\frac{1}{10}$ of 80 g $\frac{1}{10}$ of 100 h $\frac{1}{10}$ of 120

2 Work out these hundredths.

a $\frac{1}{100}$ of 500 b $\frac{1}{100}$ of 700 c $\frac{1}{100}$ of 400 d $\frac{1}{100}$ of 800

Challenge 2

1 Work out these tenths.

a $\frac{5}{10}$ of 30 b $\frac{7}{10}$ of 90 c $\frac{4}{10}$ of 50 d $\frac{9}{10}$ of 70

e $\frac{3}{10}$ of 140 f $\frac{6}{10}$ of 150 g $\frac{2}{10}$ of 180 h $\frac{3}{10}$ of 240

2 Work out these hundredths.

a $\frac{3}{100}$ of 400 b $\frac{6}{100}$ of 500 c $\frac{35}{100}$ of 300 d $\frac{41}{100}$ of 700

Challenge 3

1 Work out these tenths.

a $\frac{7}{10}$ of 610 b $\frac{3}{10}$ of 770 c $\frac{8}{10}$ of 560 d $\frac{5}{10}$ of 700

e $\frac{3}{10}$ of 940 f $\frac{2}{10}$ of 1320 g $\frac{4}{10}$ of 1250 h $\frac{6}{10}$ of 1430

2 Work out these hundredths.

a $\frac{6}{100}$ of 2500 b $\frac{8}{100}$ of 3400 c $\frac{7}{100}$ of 4000 d $\frac{5}{100}$ of 6700

Fraction problems

Solve fraction problems to calculate quantities including non-unit fractions

Challenge 1

1 Harvey orders a small milkshake. It holds 300 ml. He drinks a $\frac{1}{3}$ of it but then his brother drinks the rest. How much did Harvey drink?

2 For lunch, the cook is making 200 pizzas. Unfortunately, she burns $\frac{1}{5}$ of them. How many will she be able to serve up?

3 Harvey needs to spend 40 minutes doing his homework. He has spent $\frac{1}{8}$ of the time working out what he needs to do. How much time does he have left?

Challenge 2

1 Mr Smith is 160 cm tall. His brother is $\frac{7}{8}$ as tall as him. How tall is his brother?

2 Skateboards cost £81 in one shop. In another shop they are only $\frac{7}{9}$ of the price. How much do they cost there?

3 Harvey collects 256 conkers. He loses $\frac{3}{8}$ of them on his way home. How many does he have left?

4 A café sells milkshakes in two sizes, small and large. The small milkshake is 360 ml. The large milkshake is $\frac{2}{3}$ more. What is the size of the large milkshake?

Challenge 3

1 In the café, Harvey and his friend buy a small and a large milkshake. Harvey has drunk $\frac{3}{4}$ of his 360 ml shake and his friend has drunk $\frac{2}{3}$ of his 480 ml shake. Who has drunk the most?

2 Mr Smith is growing an enormous pumpkin. He weighs it every week. Last week it weighed 112 kg. This week it is $\frac{4}{7}$ heavier. What does it weigh this week?

3 When the local football team last played at home, the stadium was full. It can hold 4000 fans. $\frac{7}{10}$ of the spectators were the home fans and the rest were away fans. How many fans came to support the home team?

Kilometres and metres

Convert between kilometres and metres and record lengths using decimals

Challenge 1

Copy and complete the table. The first one has been done for you.

1·0 km	0·5 km	0·1 km	___ km	0·3 km	___ km	0·9 km
1000 m	___ m	___ m	800 m	___ m	___ m	___ m
1 km	$\frac{1}{2}$ km	$\frac{1}{10}$ km	$\frac{8}{10}$ km	___ km	$\frac{4}{10}$ km	___ km

Challenge 2

1 Write these distances in metres.

> **Example**
> 2·7 km = 2000 m + 700 m
> = 2700 m

a 3·6 km   b 5·5 km   c 8·9 km   d 10·2 km   e 12·8 km   f 15·4 km

2 Write these distances in kilometres.

> **Example**
> 6400 m = 6 km 400 m
> = 6·4 km

a 4800 m   b 7200 m   c 5600 m   d 9100 m   e 8300 m   f 11 200 m

3 Write these distances in order, starting with the shortest.

1690 m   1·7 km   1 km 960 m   1·9 km   1906 m   1·6 km

4 The table shows how far each hiker walked in 1 hour.

   a Who walked the furthest distance in 1 hour?

   b How many metres was Joe ahead of Len?

   c How many metres was Mike behind Harry?

Hiker	Distance
Harry	5·8 km
Joe	5 km 750 m
Len	$5\frac{1}{2}$ km
Mike	5400 m

Challenge 3

The length of each rectangular caravan park is double its width.
Find the length and perimeter of each caravan park if they have widths of:

a 70 m   b 0·2 km   c 160 m   d $\frac{1}{4}$ km

DIY measurements

Convert from larger to smaller units and record lengths using decimals

allenge 1

Copy and complete.

Example
9 cm = 90 mm

a ◯ m = 500 cm   b 5 cm = ● mm   c ● m = 5000 mm

d 8 m = ● cm   e 8 cm = ● mm   f 8 m = ◯ mm

g 0·5 m = ● cm   h 0·5 cm = ◯ mm   i ● m = 500 mm

allenge 2

1 Write these lengths as metres using decimals.

a 40 cm   b 60 cm   c 90 cm   d 250 cm

e 380 cm   f 500 mm   g 800 mm   h 900 mm

2 Draw a triangle relationship for these lengths.

a 300 mm b 60 cm   c 0·5 m

d 700 mm e 80 cm   f 2·4 m

Example

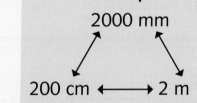

2000 mm

200 cm ⟷ 2 m

3 Write these lengths of wood in centimetres.

Example
7·3 m = 730 cm

a 4·2 m   b 8·1 m   c 5·7 m   d 3·9 m

4 Write these widths of tiles in millimetres.

Example
1·1 m = 1100 mm

a 0·6 m   b 1·3 m   c 2·8 m   d 3·5 m

hallenge 3

A window has 6 panes of glass each measuring 600 mm by 300 mm.
What is the height and width of the window in metres?

Fixing the fence in metres

Estimate and compare length and round numbers using measuring tapes

Challenge 1

Write the length shown by each nail:

a   in millimetres

b   to the nearest centimetre

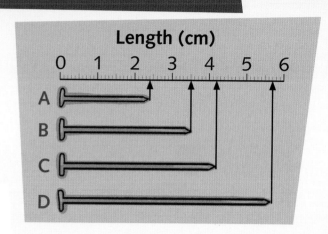

Challenge 2

1 Round the length shown by each arrow:

a   to the nearest centimetre   b   to the nearest 10 centimetres

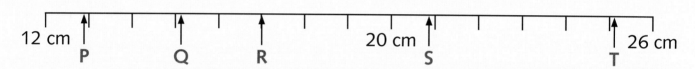

2 Estimate then work out in metres the distance between:

a   posts A and C   b   posts B and D   c   posts A and D

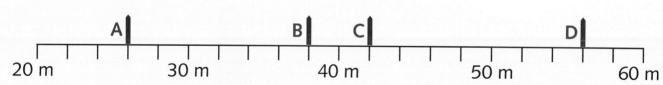

3 The table shows the length of one roll of Farmer Fraser's wire mesh. Copy and complete the table for his rolls of wire mesh with these lengths:

Length of roll of wire mesh	Rounded to nearest:	
	10 cm	metre
A 472 cm	470 cm	5 m
B		

B   274 cm   C   742 cm   D   427 cm   E   724 cm   F   247 cm

Challenge 3

Farmer Fraser needs exactly 12 m of wire mesh to complete his fence. He wants to finish the job without wasting too much of his stock of wire mesh. Which three rolls from his stock of wire mesh should he use? Give a reason for your answer.

On the map measures

Calculate different measures of length using decimals to one place

allenge 1

Look at the map then write the shortest distance between these places using decimals.

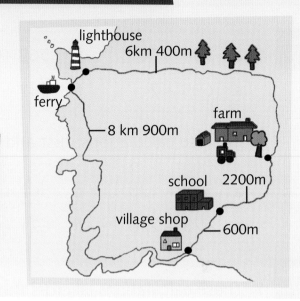

a   village shop to ferry

b   ferry to school

c   school to farm

d   farm to lighthouse

e   lighthouse to village shop

Key

~ Route

~ Seashore

---

allenge 2

1   The lighthouse is 60·9 metres tall. The height of the school building is 20 m 30 cm.

a   What is the difference in height between the two buildings?

b   How many times taller is the lighthouse than the school building?

2   Fiona lives on the farm. How far, in kilometres, does she cycle to and from school:

a   in one day?   b   in one school week?

3   What is the total distance from the ferry, past the village shop and school to the farm?

---

hallenge 3

Copy the number line below and mark the distance each cyclist is from the lighthouse.

Sam	400 m behind Pat
Nico	$\frac{1}{2}$ km ahead of Sam
Jo	$\frac{3}{10}$ km behind Nico
Pat	0·3 km from the lighthouse

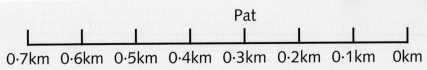

Pat

0·7km   0·6km   0·5km   0·4km   0·3km   0·2km   0·1km   0km

Adding mentally

Use mental methods for addition

 Challenge 1

1
a   534 + 50
b   568 + 9
c   527 + 400
d   672 + 40

e   695 + 7
f   742 + 80
g   382 + 600
h   861 + 90

2 In these calculations, first add the 100s and then the 10s.

a   528 + 130
b   562 + 150
c   591 + 210
d   645 + 260

e   673 + 220
f   621 + 290
g   704 + 340
h   815 + 360

 Challenge 2

1 These calculations all cross the 1000 boundary.

a   972 + 80
b   953 + 90
c   997 + 8
d   626 + 500

e   966 + 50
f   512 + 700
g   948 + 70
h   999 + 40

2 In these calculations, first add the 100s and then the 10s.

a   975 + 130
b   843 + 250
c   961 + 270
d   982 + 320

e   1005 + 340
f   1073 + 490
g   1178 + 420
h   1259 + 480

 Challenge 3

1 Choose your strategy to work out these calculations.

a   1276 + 370
b   1298 + 340
c   1382 + 360
d   1404 + 420

e   1439 + 450
f   1591 + 370
g   2235 + 410
h   2638 + 530

2 In these calculations, first add the 100s, then the 10s and then the 1s.

a   1150 + 365
b   1270 + 424
c   1320 + 487
d   1390 + 538

e   1450 + 527
f   1610 + 634
g   1860 + 682
h   2180 + 728

Subtracting mentally

Use mental methods for subtraction

1 **a** 567 – 40 **b** 581 – 7 **c** 624 – 60 **d** 649 – 500

   e 662 – 70 **f** 735 – 8 **g** 853 – 400 **h** 722 – 50

2 In these calculations, first subtract the 100s and then the 10s.

   a 643 – 120 **b** 657 – 180 **c** 682 – 230 **d** 716 – 140

   e 745 – 220 **f** 757 – 270 **g** 872 – 250 **h** 838 – 340

1 **a** 1286 – 50 **b** 1239 – 60 **c** 1373 – 8 **d** 1351 – 200

   e 1426 – 60 **f** 1479 – 300 **g** 1532 – 80 **h** 1683 – 600

2 In these calculations, first subtract the 100s and then the 10s.

   a 1352 – 140 **b** 1225 – 170 **c** 1443 – 190 **d** 1462 – 240

   e 1526 – 310 **f** 1588 – 340 **g** 1537 – 420 **h** 1683 – 490

1 Choose your strategy to work out these calculations.

   a 1684 – 560 **b** 1762 – 420 **c** 1873 – 360 **d** 1627 – 470

   e 1712 – 390 **f** 1805 – 430 **g** 2067 – 240 **h** 2251 – 270

2 In these calculations, first subtract the 100s, then the 10s and then the 1s.

   a 1480 – 261 **b** 1590 – 342 **c** 1630 – 475 **d** 1680 – 543

   e 1470 – 582 **f** 1860 – 634 **g** 2080 – 312 **h** 2150 – 238

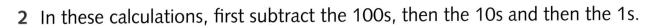

Writing 2-step problems

Write 2-step problems in contexts, deciding which operations and methods to use and why

Challenge 1

1 Write a 1-step word problem for each of these calculations and work it out.

    a 237 + 80   **b** 548 + 240   **c** 752 – 70   **d** 871 – 400

2 Ask your partner to work out the answers to two of your problems. Check if they got them right.

Challenge 2

1 Write a 2-step word problem for each of these calculations and work it out.

    a 428 + 260 + 345   **b** 862 – 300 – 360   **c** 1220 – 530 + 375

2 Ask your partner to work out the answers to two of your problems. Check if they got them right.

3 Now make up four calculations of your own and write a two-step word problem for each. Remember to use numbers that can be calculated mentally.

    a   +   +   =   **b**   –   –   =

    c   +   –   =   **d**   +   +   =

Challenge 3

1 Make up four calculations of your own and write a two-step word problem for each. Remember to use numbers that can be calculated mentally.

    a   ×   +   =   **b**   ÷   –   =

    c   ×   –   =   **d**   +   ÷   =

2 Ask your partner to work out the answers to your problems. Check if they got them right.

Written addition (3)

- Add numbers with up to 4 digits using the formal written method of columnar addition
- Estimate and use inverse operations to check answers to a calculation

 Challenge 1

Estimate the answer to these calculations and then work them out.

a 573 + 154	b 438 + 357	c 641 + 329	d 684 + 253
e 564 + 461	f 748 + 235	g 752 + 624	h 834 + 741
i 576 + 722	j 825 + 642	k 538 + 465	l 472 + 485

Challenge 2

1 Estimate the answer to these calculations and then work out them out.

a 1273 + 1349	b 1625 + 1535	c 2718 + 1627	d 2285 + 2476
e 3629 + 2446	f 3277 + 2188	g 4831 + 2543	h 4065 + 1367
i 3802 + 2458	j 4444 + 2739	k 5382 + 4598	l 6052 + 2983

2 Choose four of the calculations and check your answers using the inverse operation.

Challenge 3

1 Estimate the answer to these calculations and then work them out.

a 2571 + 1619	b 2287 + 2943	c 3695 + 1536	d 3483 + 2748
e 4726 + 3787	f 4473 + 4689	g 5784 + 3857	h 4962 + 4659
i 7699 + 1877	j 6837 + 2855	k 7367 + 2908	l 5826 + 6391

2 Choose four of the calculations and check your answers using the inverse operation.

Written addition (4)

- Add numbers with up to 4 digits using the formal written method of columnar addition
- Estimate and use inverse operations to check answers to a calculation

Challenge 1

1 Estimate the answers to these calculations, then work them out.

    a 562 + 243   **b** 627 + 281   **c** 593 + 342   **d** 426 + 447

2 These calculations add up to more than 1000.

    a 649 + 624   **b** 753 + 552   **c** 617 + 748   **d** 863 + 692

Challenge 2

1 Estimate the answers to these calculations, then work them out.

    a 2641 + 2419   **b** 3627 + 1782   **c** 2836 + 2085   **d** 3525 + 2647

    e 2371 + 3159   **f** 3628 + 2753   **g** 4183 + 2907   **h** 5351 + 3829

2 Now estimate the answers to these calculations, then work them out.

    a 4763 + 2578   **b** 3384 + 4839   **c** 3962 + 2159   **d** 4295 + 3827

Challenge 3

1 Estimate the answers to these calculations, then work them out.

    a 6276 + 2845   **b** 5395 + 3716   **c** 4876 + 2978   **d** 5075 + 3935

2 Check your calculations using the inverse operation.

3 Can you think of a more efficient way than the written method for working out the answer to this calculation: 2999 + 2999?

Written subtraction (3)

- Subtract numbers with up to 4 digits using the formal written method of columnar subtraction
- Estimate and use inverse operations to check answers to a calculation

Challenge 1

a 628 – 354	b 781 – 426	c 677 – 283	d 706 – 324
e 643 – 281	f 866 – 292	g 870 – 354	h 892 – 565
i 967 – 683	j 992 – 755	k 849 – 372	l 851 – 537

Challenge 2

1 Write an estimate for these calculations before you work them out.

a 3673 – 1835	b 3827 – 2448	c 4346 – 1571	d 4386 – 2197
e 5184 – 2358	f 6396 – 4759	g 7826 – 4188	h 7069 – 2371
i 7176 – 5338	j 7275 – 4444	k 8627 – 4708	l 8642 – 3266

2 Choose four of your calculations and check your answers using the inverse operation.

Challenge 3

1 Write an estimate for these calculations before you work them out.

a 7738 – 3819	b 7628 – 5189	c 7364 – 6715	d 8672 – 3781
e 8267 – 4598	f 8461 – 2783	g 9363 – 2495	h 9532 – 4955

2 Choose four of your calculations and check your answers using the inverse operation.

3 Can you think of a more efficient way than the written method for working out the answer to this calculation: 3999 – 1001?

Written subtraction (4)

- Subtract numbers with up to 4 digits using the formal written method of columnar subtraction
- Estimate and use inverse operations to check answers to a calculation

Challenge 1

| a | 2372 – 1541 | b | 2635 – 1853 | c | 3462 – 1358 | d | 4276 – 2628 |

| e | 4037 – 1564 | f | 4183 – 2605 | g | 4286 – 1493 | h | 4436 – 2177 |

| i | 5862 – 2924 | j | 5387 – 2839 | k | 5063 – 2235 | l | 5275 – 3428 |

Challenge 2

1 Write an estimate for these calculations before you work them out.

| a | 5287 – 2498 | b | 5295 – 2497 | c | 5826 – 1958 | d | 6328 – 3269 |

| e | 6284 – 2596 | f | 6752 – 4873 | g | 7431 – 3658 | h | 7532 – 2765 |

| i | 7444 – 3777 | j | 7115 – 4227 | k | 8396 – 4598 | l | 8175 – 6486 |

2 Choose four of your calculations and check your answers using the inverse operation.

Challenge 3

1 Write an estimate for these calculations before you work them out.

| a | 7749 – 3830 | b | 7639 – 5200 | c | 7375 – 6726 | d | 8683 – 3792 |

| e | 8278 – 4609 | f | 8472 – 2794 | g | 9374 – 2506 | h | 9543 – 4966 |

| i | 9736 – 1857 | j | 9236 – 5877 | k | 8664 – 4788 | l | 8267 – 3690 |

2 Choose four of your calculations and check your answers using the inverse operation.

3 Can you think of a more efficient way than the written method for working out the answer to this calculation: 5000 – 1999?

4 What other 3- or 4-digit calculations might be done more efficiently a different way?

Football problems

Solve 2-step problems in contexts, deciding which operations and methods to use and why

1 At the football match, 463 fans are buying a cup of tea and 254 fans are buying coffee. How many people are buying a hot drink?

2 637 fans have arrived so far. 451 of these are supporting the home team. How many are supporting the away team?

3 382 fans are in one part of the football ground and then another 140 arrive. How many fans are there now?

4 £275 is spent on hot dogs and £443 is spent on burgers. How much money was spent altogether?

1 1748 fans are sitting in one part of the football ground, 1325 in another part and 1583 in another. How many altogether?

2 The snack stall takes £3450. £890 was spent on drinks, £1650 was spent on cooked food and the rest was spent on cold food. How much was spent on cold food?

3 Out of 4820 fans, 1884 are men, 1798 are women and the rest are children. How many children were at the match?

4 3896 fans have arrived so far, then 2010 more arrive and then a further 2600. How many altogether?

1 The fans like to wear hats and scarves to support their team. Out of 5400 fans, 2150 are wearing hats only, 1890 are wearing scarves only and the rest are wearing both. How many fans are wearing a hat and a scarf?

2 The Snack Stall starts the day with 5870 hot dogs to sell. After an hour, it has 3276 left and after 2 hours, it has 1085 left. How many hot dogs were sold?

3 3874 fans are sitting down, 4759 are standing and 1673 are away from their seats getting food. How many fans altogether?

Sports bar charts

Interpret and present discrete data using scaled bar charts

You will need:
- squared paper
- ruler

Challenge 1

1 Year 4 voted for their favourite after school clubs. The tally chart shows the results.

Copy and complete the frequency table using the data in the tally chart.

Club	Number of votes
Art	IIII II
Chess	IIII
Drama	IIII I
Football	IIII IIII
ICT	IIII IIII II

Club	Frequency
Art	
Chess	
Drama	
Football	
ICT	

2 Copy and complete the bar chart using the data in the table.

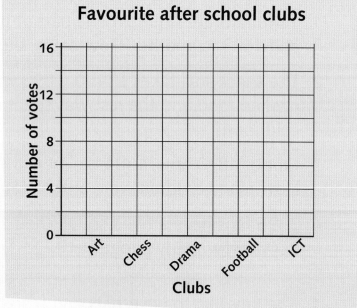

Favourite after school clubs

Number of votes: 16, 12, 8, 4, 0

Clubs: Art, Chess, Drama, Football, ICT

3 Which club is:

  a the most popular?

  b the least popular?

4 How many more children voted for ICT than:

  a Art?   **b** Drama?

5 How many votes were there altogether?

36

The local sports centre made this pictogram to show the number of people taking part in these activities on one evening.

You will need:
- squared paper
- ruler

Numbers of people taking part in sports activities

Bowls 5-a-side Judo Badminton Swimming

Key 10 people

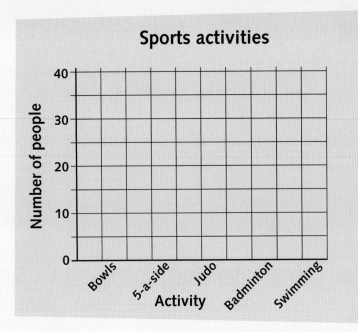

Sports activities

Number of people

40
30
20
10
0

Bowls 5-a-side Judo Badminton Swimming

Activity

1 Copy and complete the bar chart using the data in the pictogram.

2 Which activity is:

  a the most popular? b the least popular?

3 How many more people played bowls than:

  a 5-a-side? b Badminton?

4 How many fewer people took the Judo class than went to the swimming pool?

 Challenge 3

Jessica is training for a race.

  a Describe her training schedule for weeks one to six.

  b Can you think of a reason why there was a fall in the number of miles she ran in week seven?

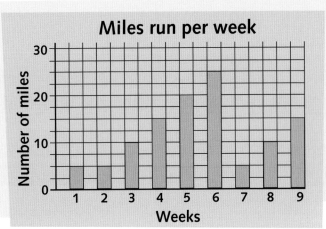

Miles run per week

Number of miles

30
20
10
0

1 2 3 4 5 6 7 8 9

Weeks

School time graphs

Interpret and present continuous data in simple time graphs

Challenge 1 The table shows the temperature in Tim's classroom on one day.

You will need:
• squared paper
• ruler

Time	Temperature (°C)
9:00 a.m.	16
10:00 a.m.	18
11:00 a.m.	20
12:00 noon	20
1:00 p.m.	22
2:00 p.m.	21
3:00 p.m.	19

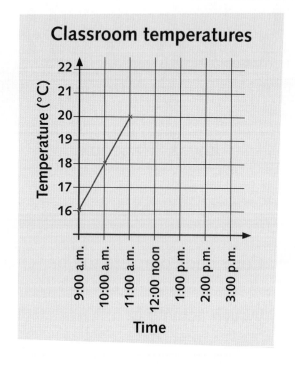

1 Copy and complete the time graph.

a Mark each point on the graph using a cross.

b Join the crosses using straight lines to make your time graph.

2 At what time was the room temperature:

a at its warmest?

b at its coolest?

3 Write two times when the temperature was the same.

4 After what time did the temperature in the room begin to fall?

1 The table shows the temperature outside on one day.
Use the information in the table to complete the time graph.

Time	Temperature
9:00 a.m.	6°C
10:00 a.m.	8°C
11:00 a.m.	10°C
12:00 noon	13°C
1:00 p.m.	15°C
2:00 p.m.	14°C
3:00 p.m.	11°C

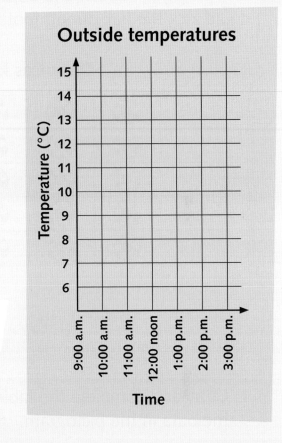

Outside temperatures

2 Write the time when it was:

a coldest outside **b** warmest outside

3 Between which two hours did the temperature:

a rise the most? **b** fall the most?

4 Between which times was the temperature
10°C or warmer?

1 The table shows the temperature in the school's kitchen.

Time	10:30 a.m.	11:00 a.m.	11:30 a.m.	12:00 noon	12:30 p.m.	1:00 p.m.
Temp. in °C	16	18	23	25	20	17

a Describe how the temperature in the kitchen changed between 10:30 a.m.
and 1:00 p.m.

b What was the approximate temperature in the kitchen at 11:45 a.m.?

Football pictograms and bar charts

Solve problems using data presented in scaled pictograms, bar charts and tables

Challenge 1

The pictogram shows the distance the players in the school's football team could kick the ball during football practice.

Distances kicked by school's football team

Distances kicked in practice		Number of players							
20 m	⚽	⚽	◖						
25 m	⚽	⚽	⚽	⚽	⚽				
30 m	⚽	⚽	⚽	⚽	⚽	⚽	⚽	◖	
35 m	⚽	⚽	⚽	⚽	⚽	⚽			
40 m	⚽	⚽	⚽	⚽					

Number of players

Key ⚽ 2 players ◖ 1 player

1 Copy and complete the table below using the data in the pictogram.

Distance	Number of players
20 m	
25 m	
30 m	
35 m	
40 m	

2 What was the maximum distance most players could kick the football?

3 a How many players could not kick the football as far as 30 m?

 b How many players could kick the football further than 30 m?

4 How many players attended the school's football practice?

The bar chart shows the number of goals scored by the school's top five players during the season.

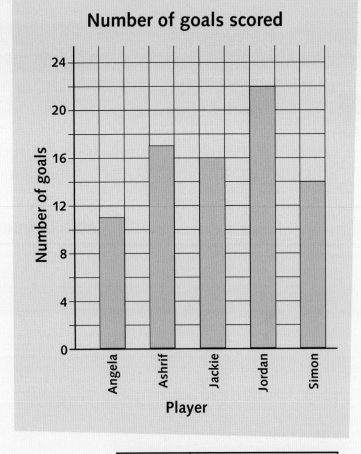

Number of goals scored

1 Using the data in the bar chart, copy and complete the table.

2 a Who was the top scorer for the football season?

b How many more goals did Ashrif score than Angela?

c How many goals did Jackie and Jordan score between them?

d How many fewer goals did Simon score than Jordan?

e Jordan scored 14 penalty goals. How many of his goals were not penalty goals?

f What was the total number of goals scored by all 5 players?

Player	Number of goals
Angela	
Ashrif	
Jackie	
Jordan	
Simon	

Work with a partner.

• Take 20 turns each to spin the spinner and make a tally mark for each goal scored.

• Count the tally marks and complete the frequency column in the table.

• Draw a bar chart using the data from the frequency table.

• Write three questions about the bar chart for your partner to answer.

You will need:

• Resource 46: Football spinner
• paper clip and pencil – for the spinner
• squared paper

Holiday in Orlando

Solve problems using data presented in simple time graphs

 Challenge 1

The Barclay family flew from London and landed at Tampa Airport in Florida. The flight took 8 hours. The graph shows the temperature in the cabin of the plane during their flight.

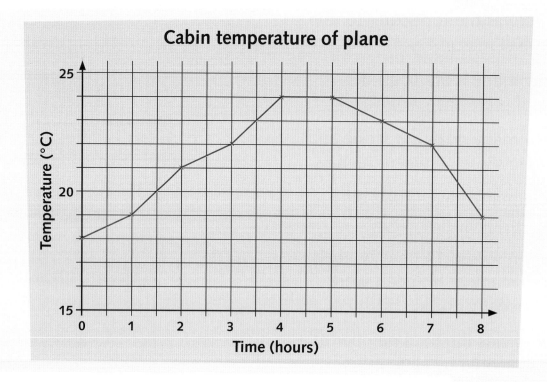

Cabin temperature of plane

Temperature (°C) vs Time (hours)

1 What was the temperature in the cabin of the plane when:

   a it took off from London?   **b** it landed at Tampa?

2 What was the temperature in the cabin:

   a at 2 hours into the flight?   **b** at 7 hours into the flight?

3 Between which 2 hours was the temperature in the cabin at its warmest?

4 By how many degrees Celsius did the temperature in the cabin drop between the 7th and the 8th hour of the flight?

5 What was the approximate temperature in the cabin at $3\frac{1}{2}$ hours into the flight?

At Tampa Airport, Mrs Barclay collected their hire car. The petrol gauge showed it had a full tank at 60 litres. The graph shows how much petrol was used on the 2-hour journey by car from Tampa to Orlando.

1 Copy and complete the table.

2 How many litres did the petrol gauge show:

   a at the end of 1 hour?

   b at the end of 2 hours?

Time (minutes)	Petrol (litres)
0	60
20	
40	
60	
80	
100	
120	

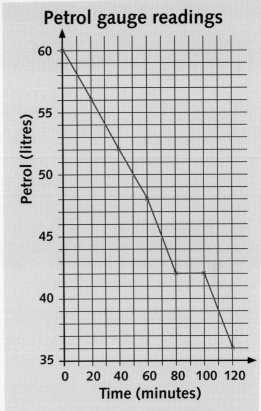

Petrol gauge readings

3 How many litres of petrol were used for the journey?

4 How many minutes into the journey did the Barclays make a short stop for refreshments?

1 The graph shows the temperature in Orlando for each day of their holiday. Between which two days did the temperature:

   a rise by 2°C?   **b** fall by 2°C?

2 Describe how the temperature changed between Thursday and Saturday.

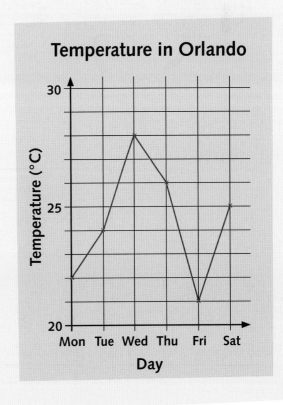

Temperature in Orlando

Multiplication HTO × O using partitioning

Use partitioning to calculate HTO × O

Challenge 1

1 a $7 \times 2 =$

   b $70 \times 2 =$

   c $700 \times 2 =$

2 a $4 \times 8 =$

   b $40 \times 8 =$

   c $400 \times 8 =$

3 a $7 \times 4 =$

   b $70 \times 4 =$

   c $700 \times 4 =$

4 a $9 \times 6 =$

   b $90 \times 6 =$

   c $900 \times 6 =$

5 a $7 \times 7 =$

   b $70 \times 7 =$

   c $700 \times 7 =$

6 a $9 \times 8 =$

   b $90 \times 8 =$

   c $900 \times 8 =$

Challenge 2

Write the answer to each of these calculations. Work the answer out mentally, using partitioning.

a 333 × 3   b 243 × 2   c 322 × 4   d 344 × 2   e 414 × 2   f 622 × 3

Challenge 3

Estimate the answer first, then partition each of these calculations to work out the answer.

a 467×4 b 468×6

c 738×4 d 383×3

e 267×9 f 691×7

g 684×5 h 794×8

i 815×9 j 609×8

> **Example**
>
> $463 \times 5 \longrightarrow 500 \times 5 = 2500$
> $= (400 \times 5) + (60 \times 5) + (3 \times 5)$
> $= 2000 \quad + 300 \quad + \quad 15$
> $= 2315$

Multiplication HTO × O using partitioning and the grid method

Use the grid method to calculate HTO × O

Challenge 1

Write the multiples of 100 that each of these numbers is between. Circle the multiple of 100 it is closest to.

Example

300 ← 386 → (400)

a 476 b 753 c 138 d 832 e 216

f 911 g 694 h 374 i 585 j 647

Challenge 2

Choose a flower pot and a flower and multiply the numbers together. Estimate your answer first, then use the grid method to work out the answer. Make six calculations. Choose different numbers each time.

Example

625 × 8 → 600 × 8 = 4800

×	600	20	5
8	4800	160	40	= 5000

453 675 486 759

637 598 477 368

7 5 6 8

4 9 3 2

Challenge 3

One of these calculations is different to the others. Can you find out why?

 468 × 4
 624 × 3
 234 × 8
 732 × 2

Multiplication HTO × O using the expanded written method

Use the expanded written method to calculate HTO × O

Count in multiples of the first number in each row.
Copy and complete each sequence.

a   25,   , 75,   ,   ,   , 200,   ,   , 300

b   40, 80,   ,   ,   , 280,   ,   ,   ,

c   60, 120,   ,   ,   ,   ,   ,   ,   , 720

d   80, 160,   ,   ,   ,   ,   , 800,   ,

e   90,   , 270,   ,   ,   , 720,   ,   , 1080

1 Estimate the answer to each calculation.

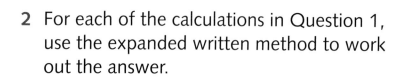

a   346 × 3   b   673 × 4   c   732 × 9   d   986 × 6

e   548 × 5   f   888 × 8   g   647 × 8   h   747 × 5

2 For each of the calculations in Question 1,
use the expanded written method to work
out the answer.

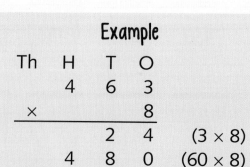

		Example		
Th	H	T	O	
	4	6	3	
×			8	
		2	4	(3 × 8)
	4	8	0	(60 × 8)
3	2	0	0	(400 × 8)
3	7	0	4	
	1			

One of the answers in Challenge 2 is the odd
one out. Can you find it? Explain how it is
different from the other answers.

Solving word problems

Solve problems and reason mathematically

Challenge 1

Copy the calculations and fill in the missing signs.

a 4 ◯ 8 = 32   b 60 = 12 ▢ 5   c 72 = 9 ▢ 8   d 15 ● 3 = 12

e 64 ◼ 8 = 8   f 7 △ 8 = 15   g 32 ▲ 8 = 24   h 96 ◯ 12 = 8

Challenge 2

Choose a sports item from the pictures. Roll the 0–9 dice to find out how many of that item you will buy. If you roll 0 or 1, roll the dice again. Write a multiplication calculation. Estimate the answer and then work it out. Make six calculations. Choose a different sports item each time.

You will need:
• 0–9 dice

Challenge 3

Answer these questions about the sports equipment above.

a Tennis balls are sold in packs of 3. How much do 90 tennis balls cost?

b What is the difference in cost between a rugby ball and a cricket ball?

c The tennis club buys 8 tennis nets, 8 tennis racquets and 8 sets of tennis balls. What is the total cost?

d There are 30 children in Year 4. Each child buys a pair of rugby boots. How much money is spent?

e If I buy 1 cricket bat, 2 sets of cricket stumps and 3 cricket balls, how much do I spend?

f The sports store has sold out of hockey sticks. They cost 4 times more than a set of tennis balls. What is the cost of a hockey stick?

Decimal hundredths

Understand the place value of hundredths

Challenge 1

1 Count the hundredths that are shaded blue and record them as a fraction and a decimal fraction.

a   b   c   d

Example

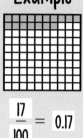

$$\frac{17}{100} = 0.17$$

2 Copy the number line and write the fractions and decimal fractions.

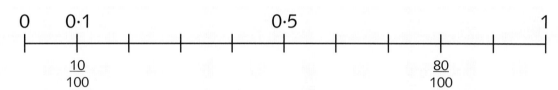

Challenge 2

1 Write the decimal fraction that is of equal value to these fractions.

a $\frac{7}{100}$ b $\frac{18}{100}$ c $\frac{22}{100}$ d $\frac{48}{100}$ e $\frac{56}{100}$ f $\frac{63}{100}$ g $\frac{76}{100}$ h $\frac{81}{100}$

2 Write these amounts as a decimal fraction.

a 26p b 37p c 44p d 57p e 65p f 77p g 84p h 99p

Challenge 3

1 What is the decimal fraction that is of equal value to these mixed numbers?

a $1\frac{34}{100}$ b $2\frac{48}{100}$ c $2\frac{81}{100}$ d $3\frac{75}{100}$ e $4\frac{3}{100}$ f $4\frac{95}{100}$ g $5\frac{72}{100}$ h $5\frac{83}{100}$

2 Write the approximate values as decimal hundredths for the arrows marked on the number line.

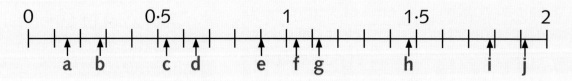

Comparing decimals (2)

Compare numbers with two decimal places

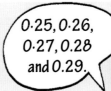
0.25, 0.26, 0.27, 0.28 and 0.29.

Challenge 1

Count on in hundredths for five numbers from these decimals.

a 0·13   b 0·46   c 1·25   d 2·76   e 3·88

f 3·59   g 4·01   h 4·38   i 4·72   j 5·09

Challenge 2

1 Write these decimal numbers in order, smallest to largest.

a 1·35, 1·63, 1·82, 1·15, 1·27   b 2·82, 2·16, 2·44, 2·19, 2·95

c 3·84, 3·27, 3·38, 3·15, 3·29   d 3·38, 3·32, 3·11, 3·89, 3·71

2 Write the decimal numbers that are one hundredth smaller and one hundredth larger than these numbers.

a 2·13   b 2·69   c 2·81   d 3·04   e 3·72

Challenge 3

1 Write a decimal number in each of the spaces, keeping each set of decimals in order.

a 5·98, ___, 6·10, ___, ___, 6·50, ___, ___, ___, ___, ___, 7·25

b ___, 7·16, ___, 7·28, ___, ___, ___, 8, ___, ___, ___, ___, 9·34

c ___, ___, 8·01, ___, ___, 8·43, ___, ___, ___, ___, ___, 10·06

d ___, 9·21, ___, ___, ___, 9·99, ___, ___, ___, ___, ___, 12·68

2 Write the greater than > or less < than sign between these numbers.

a 2·65 ___ 2·78   b 2·12 ___ 2·02   c 2·10 ___ 2·16   d 3·41 ___ 3·14

e 4·83 ___ 4·38   f 5·27 ___ 5·29   g 7·62 ___ 7·25   h 9·99 ___ 9·89

Dividing by 10

Divide 1- and 2-digit numbers by 10

Challenge 1

1 Divide these numbers by 10.

     a 4   b 3   c 9   d 6

     e 1   f 7   g 2   h 8

Hint

Ones	.	tenths
5		
0	.	5

2 Complete this sentence: When a 1-digit number is divided by 10 …

Challenge 2

1 Divide these numbers by 10.

     a 26   b 18   c 42   d 59

     e 37   f 81   g 55   h 87

Hint

Tens	Ones	.	tenths
2	8		
	2	.	8

2 Complete this sentence: When a 2-digit number is divided by 10 …

Challenge 3

1 Work out these calculations.

     a $63 \div 10$ b $98 \div 10$ c $5 \div 10$ d $62 \div 10$

     e $59 \div 10$ f $77 \div 10$ g $46 \div 10$ h $15 \div 10$

2 Apply the rule for dividing by 10 to these 3-digit numbers.

     a 145   b 186

     c 256   d 374

     e 598   f 601

Hint

Hundreds	Tens	Ones	.	tenths
2	6	3		
	2	6	.	3

3 Complete this sentence: When a 3-digit number is divided by 10 …

Dividing by 100

Divide 1- and 2-digit numbers by 100

1 Divide these numbers by 100.

| a | 4 | b | 3 | c | 9 | d | 6 |
| e | 1 | f | 7 | g | 2 | h | 8 |

Hint

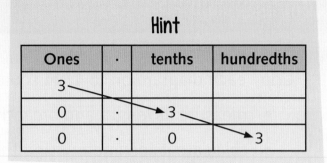

Ones	.	tenths	hundredths
3			
0	.	3	
0	.	0	3

2 Complete this sentence: When a 1-digit number is divided by 100 …

challenge 2

1 Divide these numbers by 100.

| a | 43 | b | 27 | c | 35 | d | 57 |
| e | 81 | f | 74 | g | 62 | h | 94 |

Hint

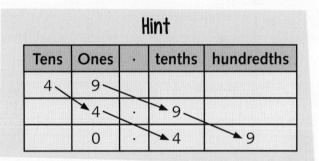

Tens	Ones	.	tenths	hundredths
4	9			
	4	.	9	
	0	.	4	9

2 Complete this sentence: When a 2-digit number is divided by 100 …

challenge 3

1 Work out these calculations.

| a | 39 ÷ 100 | b | 7 ÷ 100 | c | 28 ÷ 100 | d | 99 ÷ 100 |
| e | 84 ÷ 100 | f | 71 ÷ 100 | g | 65 ÷ 100 | h | 53 ÷ 100 |

2 Apply the rule for dividing by 100 to these 3-digit numbers.

a	172	b	385
c	391	d	574
e	658	f	701

Hint

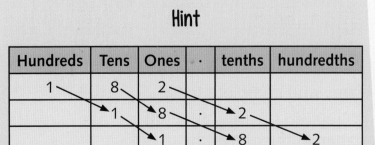

Hundreds	Tens	Ones	.	tenths	hundredths
1	8	2			
	1	8	.	2	
		1	.	8	2

Perimeter of rectangles

Measure and calculate the perimeter of rectangles using the rule P = 2(a + b)

Challenge 1

Copy each diagram on to 1 cm squared paper then:

- measure its length and breadth
- calculate its perimeter using the rule
  perimeter = twice (length plus breadth)

You will need:
- ruler
- 1 cm squared paper

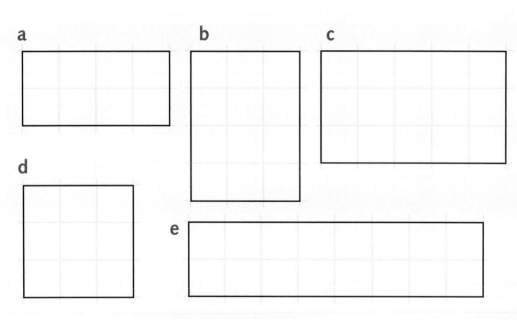

a

b

c

d

e

Example

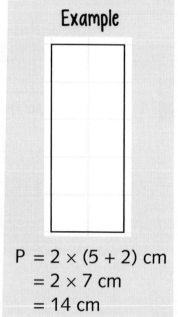

P = 2 × (5 + 2) cm
= 2 × 7 cm
= 14 cm

Challenge 2

Use the rule from Challenge 1 to find the perimeter of these rectangular fields.

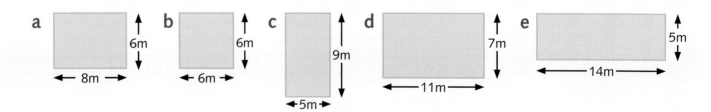

a 6m, 8m   b 6m, 6m   c 9m, 5m   d 7m, 11m   e 5m, 14m

Challenge 3

Copy and complete these rectangles on 1 cm squared paper so they have the perimeters given.

a P = 24 cm   b P = 18 cm   c P = 20 cm

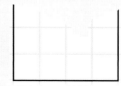

52

Counting squares for area

Find the area of rectangles by counting squares

You will need:
• centicubes

 Challenge 1

Write the number of centicubes you need to cover each rectangle.

a b c d

 Challenge 2

1 Find the area of each rectangle by counting the number of squares.

A   B   C   D

E   F

2 Which rectangle has:

a the smallest area?

b the greatest area?

c half the area of rectangle D?

d an area 2 squares less than rectangle E?

 Challenge 3

1 Use interlocking squares to make the four shapes below.

2 Fit the shapes together to make a rectangle 5 units by 4 units.

3 Copy the rectangle on to 1 cm squared paper.

4 Use coloured pencils to show how the four shapes fit together.

5 Record the area and perimeter of your rectangle.

You will need:
• interlocking squares
• 1 cm squared paper
• coloured pencils

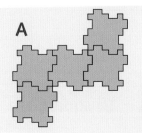 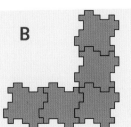 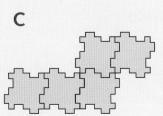 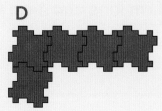

A B C D

Finding area

Find the area of rectangles and other shapes by counting squares

Challenge 1

Find the area of each shape on the pinboard by counting the number of squares.

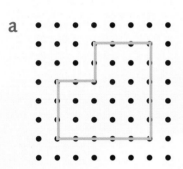

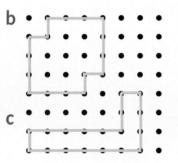

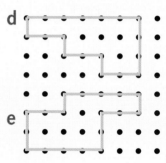

Challenge 2

Count the number of green squares in each shape and write its area. Don't forget the unit in your answers.

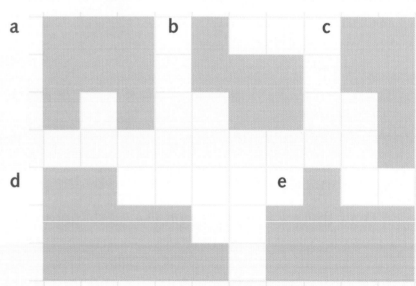

Challenge 3

Draw these rectangles on 1 cm squared paper. Below each one, write its area.

a   6 cm long and 2 cm wide

b   7 cm long and 4 cm wide

c   9 cm long and 5 cm wide

You will need:
• 1 cm squared paper
• ruler

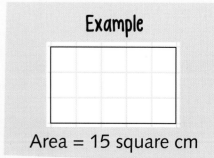

Example

Area = 15 square cm

54

Calculating area

Use multiplication to calculate the area of rectangles

Challenge 1

Each small square is 1 square cm.
Calculate the area of these rectangles.

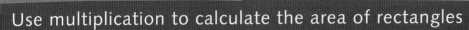

a   b   c

Example

2 rows of 2 squares
Area = 2 × 2 square cm
    = 4 square cm

Challenge 2

Each small square is 1 square cm.
Calculate the area of these rectangles.

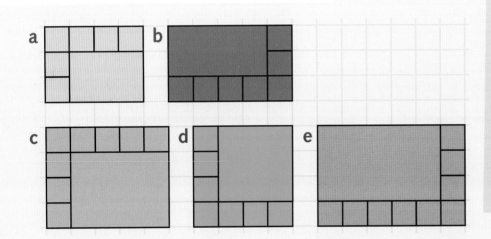

a   b
c   d   e

Example

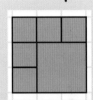

3 rows of 3 squares
Area = 3 × 3 square cm
    = 9 square cm

Challenge 3

Draw squares A to D on 1cm square dot paper.

a Find the area of each square.

b Draw the next two squares in the pattern.
   Label them E and F.

c Find the area of squares E and F.

d Predict the areas of squares G and H.

e Check your predictions by drawing the squares.

You will need:
- 1 cm square dot paper
- ruler

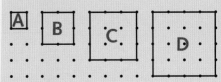

55

Maths facts

The seven steps to solving word problems

1 Read the problem carefully.   2 What do you have to find?   3 What facts are given?

4 Which of the facts do you need?   5 Make a plan.

6 Carry out your plan to obtain your answer.   7 Check your answer.

Number and place value

1000	2000	3000	4000	5000	6000	7000	8000	9000
100	200	300	400	500	600	700	800	900
10	20	30	40	50	60	70	80	90
1	2	3	4	5	6	7	8	9
0.1	0.2	0.3	0.4	0.5	0.6	0.7	0.8	0.9
0.01	0.02	0.03	0.04	0.05	0.06	0.07	0.08	0.09

Positive and negative numbers

-10 -9 -8 -7 -6 -5 -4 -3 -2 -1 0 1 2 3 4 5 6 7 8 9 10

Addition and subtraction

Number facts

+	0	1	2	3	4	5	6	7	8	9	10
0	0	1	2	3	4	5	6	7	8	9	10
1	1	2	3	4	5	6	7	8	9	10	11
2	2	3	4	5	6	7	8	9	10	11	12
3	3	4	5	6	7	8	9	10	11	12	13
4	4	5	6	7	8	9	10	11	12	13	14
5	5	6	7	8	9	10	11	12	13	14	15
6	6	7	8	9	10	11	12	13	14	15	16
7	7	8	9	10	11	12	13	14	15	16	17
8	8	9	10	11	12	13	14	15	16	17	18
9	9	10	11	12	13	14	15	16	17	18	19
10	10	11	12	13	14	15	16	17	18	19	20

+	11	12	13	14	15	16	17	18	19	20
0	11	12	13	14	15	16	17	18	19	20
1	12	13	14	15	16	17	18	19	20	
2	13	14	15	16	17	18	19	20		
3	14	15	16	17	18	19	20			
4	15	16	17	18	19	20				
5	16	17	18	19	20					
6	17	18	19	20						
7	18	19	20							
8	19	20								
9	20									

+	0	10	20	30	40	50	60	70	80	90	100
0	0	10	20	30	40	50	60	70	80	90	100
10	10	20	30	40	50	60	70	80	90	100	110
20	20	30	40	50	60	70	80	90	100	110	120
30	30	40	50	60	70	80	90	100	110	120	130
40	40	50	60	70	80	90	100	110	120	130	140
50	50	60	70	80	90	100	110	120	130	140	150
60	60	70	80	90	100	110	120	130	140	150	160
70	70	80	90	100	110	120	130	140	150	160	170
80	80	90	100	110	120	130	140	150	160	170	180
90	90	100	110	120	130	140	150	160	170	180	190
100	100	110	120	130	140	150	160	170	180	190	200

+	110	120	130	140	150	160	170	180	190	200
0	110	120	130	140	150	160	170	180	190	200
10	120	130	140	150	160	170	180	190	200	210
20	130	140	150	160	170	180	190	200	210	220
30	140	150	160	170	180	190	200	210	220	230
40	150	160	170	180	190	200	210	220	230	240
50	160	170	180	190	200	210	220	230	240	250
60	170	180	190	200	210	220	230	240	250	260
70	180	190	200	210	220	230	240	250	260	270
80	190	200	210	220	230	240	250	260	270	280
90	200	210	220	230	240	250	260	270	280	290
100	210	220	230	240	250	260	270	280	290	300

Written methods – addition

Example: 2456 + 5378

```
    2 4 5 6
  + 5 3 7 8
    7 8 3 4
      1 1
```

Written methods – subtraction

Example: 6418 – 2546

```
    5 13 11
    6̶ 4̶ 1̶ 8
  – 2 5 4 6
    3 8 7 2
```

Multiplication and division

Number facts

x	2	3	4	5	6	7	8	9	10	11	12
1	2	3	4	5	6	7	8	9	10	11	12
2	4	6	8	10	12	14	16	18	20	22	24
3	6	9	12	15	18	21	24	27	30	33	36
4	8	12	16	20	24	28	32	36	40	44	48
5	10	15	20	25	30	35	40	45	50	55	60
6	12	18	24	30	36	42	48	54	60	66	72
7	14	21	28	35	42	49	56	63	70	77	84
8	16	24	32	40	48	56	64	72	80	88	96
9	18	27	36	45	54	63	72	81	90	99	108
10	20	30	40	50	60	70	80	90	100	110	120
11	22	33	44	55	66	77	88	99	110	121	132
12	24	36	48	60	72	84	96	108	120	132	144

Written methods – multiplication

Example: 356 x 7

Partitioning

356 x 7 = (300 x 7) + (50 x 7) + (6 x 7)
= 2100 + 350 + 42
= 2492

Grid method

x	300	50	6	
7	2100	350	42	= 2492

Expanded written method

```
    3 5 6
  ×     7
      4 2   (  6 x 7)
    3 5 0   ( 50 x 7)
  2 1 0 0   (300 x 7)
  2 4 9 2
```

Formal written method

```
    3 5 6
  × ₃ ₄ 7
  2 4 9 2
```

Written methods – division

Example: 486 ÷ 9

Partitioning

486 ÷ 9 = (450 ÷ 9) + (36 ÷ 9)
= 50 + 4
= 54

Formal written method

```
      5 4
  9 ) 4 8 ³6
```

Expanded written method

```
        5 4
  9 ) 4 8 6
      4 5 0  | 50 × 9
        3 6
        3 6  | 4 × 9
          0
```

57

Fractions and decimals

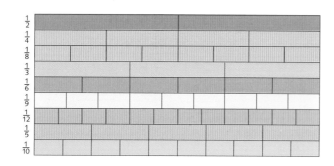

$$\frac{1}{100} = 0{\cdot}01$$

$$\frac{2}{100} = \frac{1}{50} = 0{\cdot}02$$

$$\frac{5}{100} = \frac{1}{20} = 0{\cdot}05$$

$$\frac{10}{100} = \frac{1}{10} = 0{\cdot}1$$

$$\frac{20}{100} = \frac{1}{5} = 0{\cdot}2$$

$$\frac{25}{100} = \frac{1}{4} = 0{\cdot}25$$

$$\frac{50}{100} = \frac{1}{2} = 0{\cdot}5$$

$$\frac{75}{100} = \frac{3}{4} = 0{\cdot}75$$

$$\frac{100}{100} = 1$$

Measurement

Length
1 kilometre (km) = 1000 metres (m)

0·1 km = 100 m

1 m = 100 centimetres (cm) = 1000 millimetres (mm)

0·1 m = 10 cm = 100 mm

1 cm = 10 mm

0·1 cm = 1 mm

Mass
1 kilogram (kg) = 1000 grams (g)

0·1 kg = 100 g

0·01 kg = 10 g

Capacity
1 litre (*l*) = 1000 millilitres (ml)

0·1 *l* = 100 ml

0·01 *l* = 10 ml

Time
1 year = 12 months

= 365 days

= 366 days (leap year)

1 week = 7 days

1 day = 24 hours

1 hour = 60 minutes

1 minute = 60 seconds

30 days has September, April, June and November. All the rest have 31, except February alone which has 28 days clear and 29 in each leap year.

12-hour clock 24-hour clock

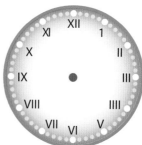

Properties of shape

2-D shapes

 circle

semi-circle

 right-angled triangle

 equilateral triangle

isosceles triangle

 scalene triangle

 square

 rectangle

 rhombus

 kite

 parallelogram

 trapezium

 pentagon

 hexagon

 heptagon

 octagon

3-D shapes

cube

cuboid

cone

cylinder

sphere

hemisphere

triangular prism

triangular-based pyramid (tetrahedron)

square-based pyramid

Angles

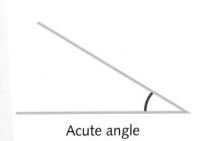

Acute angle

Right angle

Obtuse angle

Position and direction

Coordinates

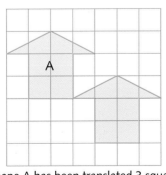

Translation

Shape A has been translated 3 squares to the right and 2 squares down.

Reflection

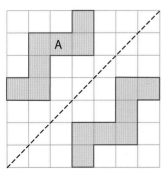

Shape A has been reflected in the diagonal line of symmetry.

59